THE LIBRARY OF PHYSICAL SCIENCE™

The Properties of Salts

Marylou Morano Kjelle

The Rosen Publishing Group's

PowerKids Press™

New York

*To my sisters and brothers-in-law, Teresa and Brian Hogan and
Jennifer and Glenn Mongold*

Published in 2007 by The Rosen Publishing Group, Inc.
29 East 21st Street, New York, NY 10010

First Edition

Editors: Joanne Randolph and Suzanne Slade
Book Design: Elana Davidian
Book Layout: Ginny Chu
Photo Researcher: Nicole Dimella

Photo Credits: Cover © John Sohlden/Visuals Unlimited; pp. 4, 8 © Tony Freeman/Photo Edit,
Inc.; p. 6 (top) Maura B. McConnell; pp. 6 (bottom), 16 © Charles D. Winters/Photo
Researchers, Inc.; p. 7 © Phototake Inc./Alamy; p. 9 © Sciencephotos/Alamy; p. 10 © J. King-
Holmes/Photo Researchers, Inc.; p. 11 © Alan Sirulnikoff/Photo Researchers, Inc.; p. 12 (top) ©
Digital Stock; p.12 (bottom) BSIP/OSF; p. 13 © Larry Stepanowicz/Visuals Unlimited; p. 14
www.istockphoto.com/Paul Cowan; p. 15 © David Young-Wolff/Photo Edit, Inc.; p. 18 © Blair
Seitz/Photo Researchers, Inc.; p. 19 © Andrew Lambert Photography/Photo Researchers, Inc.;
p. 20 www.istockphoto.com/Steven Allan; p. 21 © Karen Kasmauski/Corbis.

Library of Congress Cataloging-in-Publication Data

Kjelle, Marylou Morano.
  The properties of salts / Marylou Morano Kjelle.— 1st ed.
     p. cm. — (The library of physical science)
  Includes index.
  ISBN 1-4042-3425-X (library binding) — ISBN 1-4042-2172-7 (pbk.)
  1. Salts—Juvenile literature. 2. Matter–Properties—Juvenile literature. 3. Chemical elements—
Juvenile literature. I. Title.   II. Series.
QD189.K54 2007
546'.34—dc22
                                                    2005035720

Manufactured in the United States of America

Contents

What Is Salt?

What tastes great on your french fries and on lots of other foods? Salt, of course! There are many different types of salts besides the tiny white **crystals** you put on your food. As is everything in the world, salts are made of elements.

Table salt is found in many foods. It is also used in cooking to bring out the taste in foods.

An element is the most basic form of matter. An element cannot be broken down into simpler **substances**. There are 116 known elements. Each element is shown on a chart called the periodic table.

The Periodic Table of Elements

1	1																			2	4
H																				**He**	
Hydrogen																				Helium	

Atomic Number → **11**   **23** ← Atomic Weight

Chemical Symbol → **Na**

Sodium ← Name of Element

Atomic Number → **17**   **35** ← Atomic Weight

Chemical Symbol → **Cl**

Chlorine ← Name of Element

3 7	4 9												5 11	6 12	7 14	8 16	9 19	10 20
Li Lithium	**Be** Beryllium												**B** Boron	**C** Carbon	**N** Nitrogen	**O** Oxygen	**F** Fluorine	**Ne** Neon
11 23 **Na** Sodium	12 24 **Mg** Magnesium												13 27 **Al** Aluminum	14 28 **Si** Silicon	15 31 **P** Phosphorus	16 32 **S** Sulfur	17 35 **Cl** Chlorine	18 40 **Ar** Argon
19 39 **K** Potassium	20 40 **Ca** Calcium	21 45 **Sc** Scandium	22 48 **Ti** Titanium	23 51 **V** Vanadium	24 52 **Cr** Chromium	25 55 **Mn** Manganese	26 56 **Fe** Iron	27 59 **Co** Cobalt	28 59 **Ni** Nickel	29 64 **Cu** Copper	30 65 **Zn** Zinc	31 70 **Ga** Gallium	32 73 **Ge** Germanium	33 75 **As** Arsenic	34 79 **Se** Selenium	35 80 **Br** Bromine	36 84 **Kr** Krypton
37 85 **Rb** Rubidium	38 88 **Sr** Strontium	39 89 **Y** Yttrium	40 91 **Zr** Zirconium	41 93 **Nb** Niobium	42 96 **Mo** Molybdenum	43 98 **Tc** Technetium	44 101 **Ru** Ruthenium	45 103 **Rh** Rhodium	46 106 **Pd** Palladium	47 108 **Ag** Silver	48 112 **Cd** Cadmium	49 115 **In** Indium	50 119 **Sn** Tin	51 122 **Sb** Antimony	52 128 **Te** Tellurium	53 127 **I** Iodine	54 131 **Xe** Xenon
55 133 **Cs** Cesium	56 137 **Ba** Barium	57 139 **La** Lanthanum	72 178 **Hf** Hafnium	73 181 **Ta** Tantalum	74 184 **W** Tungsten	75 186 **Re** Rhenium	76 190 **Os** Osmium	77 192 **Ir** Iridium	78 195 **Pt** Platinum	79 197 **Au** Gold	80 201 **Hg** Mercury	81 204 **Tl** Thallium	82 207 **Pb** Lead	83 209 **Bi** Bismuth	84 209 **Po** Polonium	85 210 **At** Astatine	86 222 **Rn** Radon
87 223 **Fr** Francium	88 226 **Ra** Radium	89 227 **Ac** Actinium	104 261 **Rf** Rutherfordium	105 262 **Db** Dubnium	106 263 **Sg** Seaborgium	107 262 **Bh** Bohrium	108 265 **Hs** Hassium	109 266 **Mt** Meitnerium	110 269 **Uun** Ununilium	111 272 **Uuu** Unununium	112 277 **Uub** Ununbium	113 284 **Uut** Ununbium	114 289 **Uuq** Ununquadium	115 288 **Uup** Ununpentium	116 292 **Uuh** Ununhexium		

Lanthanide Series

58 140 **Ce** Cerium	59 141 **Pr** Praseodymium	60 144 **Nd** Neodymium	61 145 **Pm** Promethium	62 150 **Sm** Samarium	63 152 **Eu** Europium	64 157 **Gd** Gadolinium	65 159 **Tb** Terbium	66 163 **Dy** Dysprosium	67 165 **Ho** Holmium	68 167 **Er** Erbium	69 169 **Tm** Thulium	70 173 **Yb** Ytterbium	71 175 **Lu** Lutetium

Actinide Series

90 232 **Th** Thorium	91 231 **Pa** Protactinium	92 238 **U** Uranium	93 237 **Np** Neptunium	94 244 **Pu** Plutonium	95 243 **Am** Americium	96 247 **Cm** Curium	97 247 **Bk** Berkelium	98 251 **Cf** Californium	99 252 **Es** Einsteinium	100 257 **Fm** Fermium	101 258 **Md** Mendelevium	102 259 **No** Nobelium	103 262 **Lr** Lawrencium

This is the periodic table. Each element has a one- or two-letter label.
Sodium is Na and chlorine is Cl. Can you find sodium and chlorine here?

Elements are placed near other elements that are alike. Scientists call these groups families.

Table salt is made from the elements sodium and chlorine. For this reason it is also called sodium chloride.

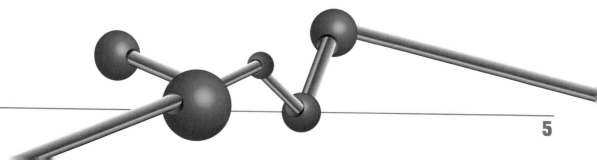

The Properties of Salt

Every element has its own physical properties. Physical properties tell you how an element looks or acts. For example, the metal called sodium is a silvery white metal. When combined with other elements, it can be used to make

Sodium is so soft it can easily be cut with a knife.

such things as other metals, paper, and glass. By itself chlorine is a yellow green gas. When it is part of a **solution**, chlorine becomes a liquid. **Compounds** that include chlorine are used to make cleaning supplies, plastics, and paints.

Chlorine is a yellow green gas, as can be seen inside this clear bottle.

Here sodium and chlorine are reacting to create salt.

When elements combine to form a salt, a new compound is made. The properties of a salt are not the same as the properties of the elements that joined to form the salt. When sodium and chlorine combine, a **chemical reaction** occurs. The result is a salt called sodium chloride. Sodium chloride is neither a metal nor a gas. Sodium chloride does not look silvery, like sodium metal, or yellow green, like chlorine gas. It does not smell, taste, or act the way either sodium metal or chlorine gas does.

Solid Salts

Everything in the world is a solid, a liquid, or a gas. A salt can be found in all three states, though it is most often seen as a solid or a liquid. The solid form of salt is the one with which we are most familiar. Solid salt is a crystal. A crystal is any solid in which the **atoms** that make it up arrange themselves in a set pattern. You might wonder what makes the atoms arrange themselves this way.

Sodium chloride is also called halite. Halite forms when salty bodies of water evaporate, or turn into a gas. When the water leaves, large crystals of salt remain.

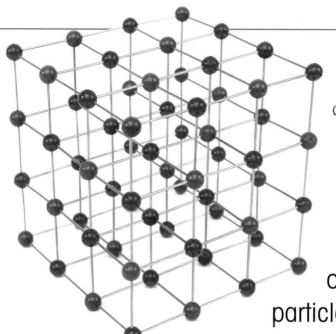

This model shows the pattern of a sodium chloride crystal. Salt crystals form cube shapes. A cube is a six-sided shape with square faces.

A salt is made of **charged** particles, or small pieces of matter, called ions. Some ions have a positive charge, and some ions have a negative charge. Negative is the opposite of positive. Just as magnets will pull toward each other if they have opposite charges, oppositely charged ions of a salt pull toward each other. This is called an ionic bond. This bond keeps the ions close together and gives a solid salt its crystal shape.

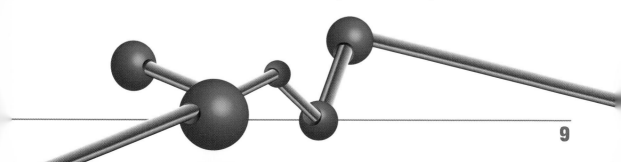

Liquid and Gaseous Salts

Just as a bowl of ice cream will melt when you add heat, a salt will also melt and become a liquid when heated. Heat gives the salt ions **energy**, and they begin to move. As they move, the bonds holding the ions together break. This allows the ions to move freely. The salt loses its crystal pattern and it becomes a liquid. The point at which a salt will turn into a liquid is called its melting point.

When metals melt, as this one has, they become liquid and can be poured.

When matter becomes a gas, such as the steam above these pots, it loses its shape and its atoms move freely.

Liquid salt becomes a gas when it is heated to its boiling point. It takes a lot of heat to break the ionic bonds that hold the crystal pattern of salt together. The melting point of sodium chloride is 1,474° F (801° C), and its boiling point is 2,669° F (1,465° C).

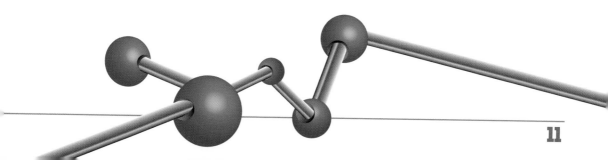

How Is Salt Made?

A salt is made when two or more elements are mixed. The elements mixed to make a salt must be an **acid** and a **base**. Acids dissolve, or break down in water. They will eat away other things, such as metals.

Lemon juice is an acid.

Another property of an acid is that it has a sour taste when dissolved in water. For example, lemon juice is an acid. A base tastes bitter. The baking soda found

Baking soda is a base.

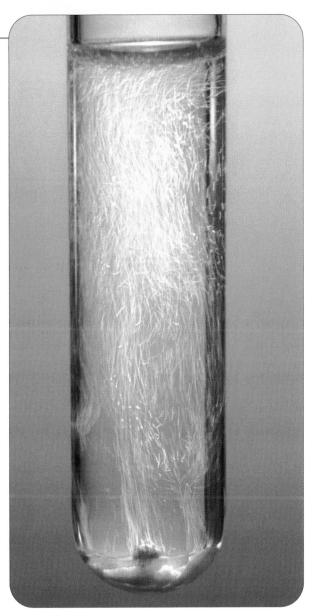

Sodium chloride is made from the base sodium hydroxide and the acid hydrochloric acid. Here we can see the reaction between hydrochloric acid and sodium bicarbonate as a salt is formed.

in your kitchen, which is also called sodium bicarbonate, is an example of a base.

When an acid and a base are mixed together, this creates water and a salt. The mixing of an acid and a base to make a salt is called neutralization. The new solution is neither an acid nor a base.

Salts and Solubility

A solution is made when one substance dissolves in another substance. Sodium chloride dissolved in water makes a solution. If you place a small amount of table salt into a glass of water, the salt will disappear. When this happens the salt is said to be soluble in water.

When the salt is placed in the water, a game of tug-of-war begins. The salt's ionic bonds fight to keep the salt in its solid crystal

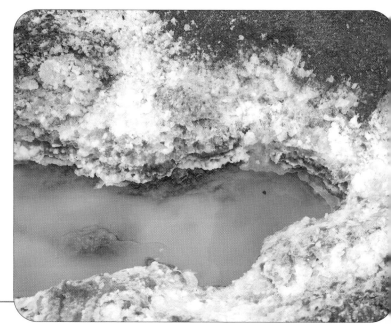

This water has a lot of salt in it. As the water evaporates, the salt crystals form again.

As this young woman pours salt into the water, the crystals will dissolve.

shape. The water tries to pull the crystal's ions apart, though. Over time the water wins. The ions that make up salt are pulled free of their crystal pattern. The salt separates into sodium ions and chloride ions. The water molecules force the ions into the solution by surrounding them on all sides.

Sodium chloride dissolves best in water. It either will not dissolve at all, or it dissolves very little in other liquids.

Salts Conduct Electricity

Electricity is a form of energy. Ions are created when a part of an atom called an **electron** leaves one atom and joins another. The movement of electrons is electricity. In order for electricity to flow, an electric **conductor** must be present. Many metals are good conductors. Salt solutions are good conductors of electricity, too. This is because they have charged ions. Once the water molecules pull some of the

Pure water does not conduct electricity. A salt solution does, though. Here a solution of the salt potassium chloride in water helps light this lightbulb.

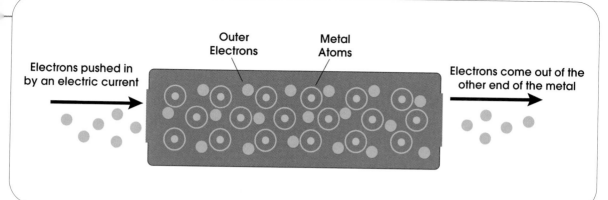

This picture shows how a conductor works. The outer electrons in a conductor move freely. As an electric current flows through the conductor, the electrons move from one atom to the next until they exit the conductor.

ions from the salt, the ions are free to move about in the water. It is these ions floating in the solution that carry the electric current.

Substances that conduct electricity when they are dissolved in water are called electrolytes. Most salts become electrolytes when they are placed in water. Therefore, most salts are good conductors of electricity. If a wire is placed into a glass that holds a salt dissolved in water, electricity can flow through the wire.

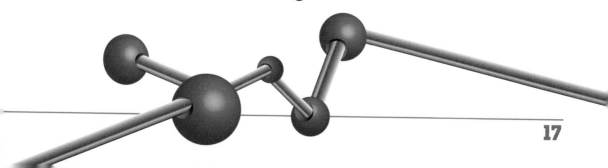

There are many different types of salts. Every kind of salt has its own properties, such as color, taste, and smell. The table salt you eat is white. Other salts made from sodium may be different colors, though. Some, such as sodium chromate, are yellow. Other salts, such as sodium dichromate, are orange. Some salts are made from mercury, a liquid metal. They can be white, gray, yellow, red, or black. Salts can also be blue, green, or they can have no color at all.

There are many different salts here. Sodium chloride is on the bottom left. To the right are two different kinds of iron sulfate. At the top is copper sulfate. Copper carbonate is on the left.

We add sodium chloride to foods, such as these pretzels, to give them a salty taste.

Because salts come in so many colors, they are often used to make dyes.

We know that sodium chloride tastes salty, but not all salts have a salty taste. Some salts are sweet, others are sour, and some are even bitter.

Different salts also have different smells. A salt usually smells like the elements of which it is made. Salts made from the gas ammonia usually smell like ammonia. Sodium chloride has no smell at all.

How Our Bodies Use Salt

Did you know that people need sodium chloride to live? Every cell in our bodies is surrounded by a solution of salt water. This solution keeps our cells healthy and allows our **nervous system** to work properly. Salt also makes sure that blood does not become too acidic or too basic. This is an important job of salt in our bodies. When salt does this job, it is called a buffer.

Most of the sodium chloride that people eat is taken from bodies of salt water, such as the Dead Sea. The Dead Sea is so salty that fish cannot live in its waters.

People all over the world need salt! Here salt is being collected at the Hon Khoi salt factory in Vietnam. Ponds are filled with seawater and then left to evaporate.

The human body needs to take in between 5 and 10 grams (.2–.4 oz) of salt each day to stay healthy. If a person went too long without taking in any salt, the body would become sick and the person could die. However, eating too much salt is unhealthy.

Both people and animals need salt, but they cannot make it or store it in their bodies. Therefore, both must take in salt from food.

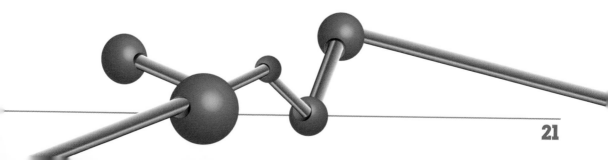

The Many Uses of Salts

Salt is used in many ways. Sodium chloride is used to make more than 14,000 things people use. We use sodium chloride to season our food and to keep it from going bad. We also use it to make leather products, soap, glass, and plastic.

We use other salts, such as calcium chloride, to dissolve snow and melt ice on our roads in the winter. A salt called calcium sulfate is used to make casts for broken bones. The fertilizers farmers use to help their crops grow are made of salts, too. Even the lotion we use to make hurting or dry skin feel better is a salt called zinc carbonate. Remember that the next time someone asks you to "please pass the salt!"

Glossary

acid (A-sid) A sour-tasting, positively charged substance that forms a salt when combined with a base in a solution.

atoms (A-temz) The smallest parts of elements that can exist either alone or with other elements.

base (BAYS) A bitter-tasting, negatively charged substance that combines with an acid to form a salt.

charged (CHARJD) Having a force like the strength of a magnet.

chemical reaction (KEH-mih-kul ree-AK-shun) The result that happens when matter is mixed with other matter to cause changes.

compounds (KOM-powndz) Two or more things combined.

conductor (kun-DUK-ter) Matter that allows current electricity to flow.

crystals (KRIS-tulz) Solids in which the molecules are arranged a fixed pattern.

electron (ih-LEK-tron) A particle inside an atom that spins around the nucleus. It has a negative charge.

energy (EH-nur-jee) The power to work or to act.

nervous system (NER-vus SIS-tum) The system of nerve fibers in people or animals.

solution (suh-LOO-shun) A mixture of two elements, one of which dissolves in the other.

substances (SUB-stan-siz) Any matter that takes up space.

Index

Web Sites

Due to the changing nature of Internet links, PowerKids Press has developed an online list of Web sites related to the subject of this book. This site is updated regularly. Please use this link to access the list:
www.powerkidslinks.com/lops/salts/